BET YOU CAN!

VICKI COBB
and KATHY DARLING

BET YOU CAN!

SCIENCE POSSIBILITIES
TO FOOL YOU

Illustrated by Stella Ormai

Lothrop, Lee & Shepard Books   New York

DEDICATED TO HARRY HOUDINI,
who knew every trick in the book

Text copyright © 1983, 1990 by Vicki Cobb and Kathy Darling
Illustrations copyright © 1983, 1990 by Stella Ormai
This edition is published by arrangement with Avon Books All rights reserved. No part of this book
may be reproduced or utilized in any form or by any means, electronic or mechanical, including
photocopying, recording or by any information storage and retrieval system, without permission in
writing from the Publisher. Inquiries should be addressed to Lothrop, Lee & Shepard Books, a division
of William Morrow & Company, Inc., 105 Madison Avenue, New York, New York 10016. Printed in
the United States of America.
First Hardcover Edition 1 2 3 4 5 6 7 8 9 10

Library of Congress Cataloging in Publication Data
Cobb, Vicki. Bet you can! : science possibilities to fool you / by Vicki Cobb and Kathy Darling :
illustrations by Stella Ormai.
———p.———cm. Summary: Describes more than sixty tricks based on scientific experiments featured in
the text. ISBN 0-688-09865-7 1. Science—Experiments—Juvenile literature. 2. Scientific recreations—Juvenile literature. [1. Science—Experiments. 2. Scientific recreations. 3. Experiments.]
I. Darling, Kathy. II. Ormai, Stella, ill. III. Title.
Q184.C478 1990 793.8—dc20

90-6690 CIP AC

CONTENTS

AGAINST ALL ODDS

Bet you can get hooked on this book after trying only one trick. Pick any page. Try any trick.

It looks like you will have to go against all odds. Your first reaction, which is only normal, is that these challenges are s-o-o-o impossible only a fool would even try. But we bet you *can* do them . . . and we're no fools!

You can't lose because these are all fixed bets. In each one the odds are stacked . . . and they are all in your favor. We guarantee you're going to win. We're betting on a sure thing when we say you'll be hooked on these "impossibles" that will send you on a surefire, perpetual winning streak.

The key to your success is science, the big puzzle-solver. Mother Nature is a great fooler. There are orderly rules of behavior. But those laws have unexpected exceptions. And they can fool you. Mother Nature has other tricks up her sleeve. Some things are not what they appear to be. And appearances can be deceiving. It has taken scientists hundreds of years to uncover some of these secrets. In these tricks we're using this "insiders'" knowledge so you can cash in on the discoveries.

Surprise yourself. Fool your friends. Amaze your teachers. With Mother Nature as your secret ally, you can make fun out of seemingly impossible situations. You're bound to have a good time. We'll bet on that!

7

1
THE HUMAN WONDER

Who is the Human Wonder? It's not Superman, Wonder Woman, or even the Incredible Hulk. It's someone with the power of science. Surprise! It's you.

You can perform "superhero" acts you didn't know were possible. We're going to reveal some of your unbelievable powers in this chapter. The Incredible Hulk may well envy your ability to hold down someone with a single thread, and you can "outsuper" Superman with secret messages sent by your blood.

The most surprising thing of all is that these talents have been there all along. But most people can't use these quirks of taste, touch, and sight without the kind of help we're going to give you. The capacity of the human mind and body has long fascinated scientists. Their testing, stressing, and pushing of the limits of the human being have led to many useful discoveries. This chapter probably will not introduce things that will make medical history. The "Human Wonders" were selected for the highest possible "fun and stun" factors . . . but this is just the beginning. . . .

ONE YARD

THE
PORTABLE
MEASURE—
—ME!

ONE HAND
4 INCHES

ONE FOOT

FOOT FEAT

Bet you can tell shoe sizes without looking at feet!

The setup: Measure the distance from your elbow to your wrist. Then measure the length of your foot.

The fix: Nobody would guess it, but the two measurements are the same. Your body has some very surprising proportions. It's hard to believe that the distance around a closed fist also is the length of your foot. Still another fooler is that the distance from fingertip to fingertip of your outstretched arms is the same as your height.

The convenience of such "portable" measuring devices led to the use of the parts of the body as linear measurements: the first knuckle of the thumb (inch), the foot, the distance from fingertip to nose (yard), and the hand (four inches), which is used to measure horses.

KEEPING THE LIDS ON

Bet you can roll your eyeballs so that you can't open your eyes!

The setup: Roll your eyeballs so that you are looking up as high as you can. Do not tilt your head backward. Now close your eyes. Keep your eyeballs in the raised position and try to open your eyes.

The fix: This is impossible. The muscles that are required to raise the eyelids are already hard at work in the opposite direction keeping the eyeballs looking upward. In fact, there are many people who can't even shut their eyes with their eyeballs rolled back. So if you are one of these, shut your eyelids and roll back your eyeballs under your closed eyelids. Now try to open your eyelids.

HOT STUFF

Bet you can taste hot peppers with your wrist!

The setup: Place a few drops of Tabasco sauce on the inside of your wrist. Wait a few minutes.

The fix: In a few minutes you will definitely feel a burning sensation on your wrist. The burning sensation is not as great as the burning sensation you would feel on your tongue, which has the most receptors for the "hot" chemicals.

In Tabasco sauce and other "hot" spices there is a chemical that triggers nerves that respond to "hotness." Be sure and wash the Tabasco sauce off your wrist with soap and water when you have finished the experiment. Hot peppers can cause irritation over a prolonged period.

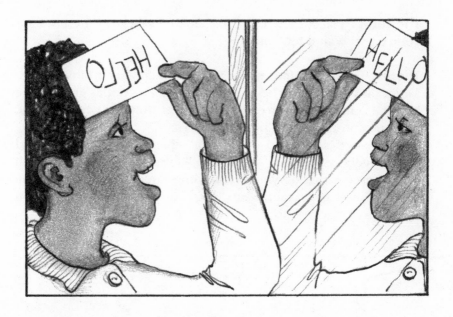

WRITE WRONG
Bet you can write backward!

The setup: Hold an index card against your forehead. Write a word on the card going from your left to your right. Imagine you are writing normally. Don't stop to think about it.

The fix: You won't be able to read what you have written unless you hold it up to a mirror. Amazing, but you have perfect mirror writing. Ordinarily you would not be able to do this, but when you hold the paper against your forehead the right and left sides of your brain get confused and a mirror or backward image of normal writing occurs. Great for making secret codes!

ONLY BY A THREAD . . .

Bet you can hold a friend on the ground with a thread!

The setup: Get a friend to lie face up on the ground. Hold the ends of a piece of thread about two feet long in your hands. Place the middle of the thread under your friend's nose. Now let your friend attempt to stand up.

The fix: The "thread victim" will have to lie helplessly on the floor. The reason? The upper lip is an extremely sensitive spot. It hurts too much to try to break a thread held there. It won't take much force to keep a good friend down.

Your friend is not the only one with a touchy upper lip. You can lead a bull around with a ring in his sensitive nose area. And cowboys subdue a wild horse with a nose string called a "twitch."

A NOSE JOB

Bet you can hang a spoon on the end of your nose!

The setup: For this trick, use any nose and any metal teaspoon. Heat the bowl of a spoon either by rubbing it in your hand or placing it in a cup of hot liquid. When the spoon is warm, tilt back your head just slightly and let the bowl of the spoon run down the top of your nose, with the handle hanging down. As you return your head to its normal position, the spoon will stick to the end of your nose and hang there. Some people have been known to "hang spoon" for several hours. Good "spoon hangers" can talk and even laugh during the experience.

The fix: We honestly don't know why this trick works. We think the spoon sticks because the heat from the metal causes the tissues of the nose to swell and conform to the shape of the spoon. But we are only guessing.

This is a stunt that some people can do the first time they try it. Others have to practice a few times before they get the "hang" of it. If you aren't one of the lucky first-timers, continue rubbing the bowl to heat it and stroking the spoon down the top of your nose. The effort is well worth it, for this is a mysterious and amusing stunt that is guaranteed to make you noticed in any restaurant.

DISJOINTED DIGIT
Bet you can make your finger hang loose!

The setup: Hold your hand with the fingers extended straight out. Bend the ring finger down at the second joint but keep the other fingers fully extended. Flick the tip of the ring finger repeatedly with the index finger of the other hand.

The fix: Weirdness reigns! The fingertip appears to be disjointed and wobbles up and down with each flick.

The bones are held together with strong ropelike connectors called ligaments, and the muscles are attached to the bones by ropelike connectors called tendons. When you bend your ring finger the ligaments and tendons holding the tip of your finger are completely relaxed. Your finger joint wobbles freely at a mere touch but you can't move it without outside help. The same phenomenon occurs with your other fingers but not to the same extent as with your ring finger. The "disjointed" fingertip doesn't work if you bend all your fingers or if you extend all your fingers straight out. Try it. Strangeness itself!

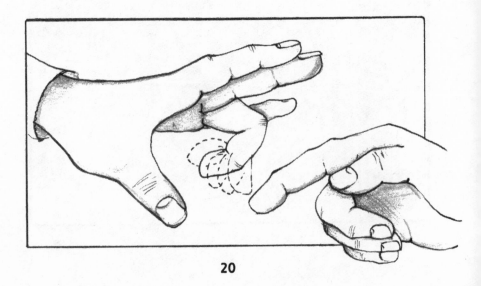

NEW MOON?

Bet you can make a full moon shrink!

The setup: This illusion has two parts: (1) Look at a full moon just after it has risen. The moon should be near the horizon. (2) Next, view the moon through a little window you make from the space between the thumb and forefingers of each hand held together. View only the moon. Don't let any of the objects on the ground enter your little viewing window.

The fix: The "shrinking moon" illusion has been known for hundreds of years. Although the ancients realized the moon seems much smaller when it is high in the sky, the reason behind this illusion still is not completely understood.

Scientists have measured our perceptions, and we see the moon as 2½ to 3½ times larger near the horizon than high in the sky. The best theory to explain this phenomenon is that the moon appears larger when it is near identifiable objects. When you remove these visual cues by blocking them out with your fingertips or by waiting until the moon is high in the sky, the moon appears to shrink. Instantly.

BLOOD TELLS!

Bet you can write a secret message on your arm without using any ink!

The setup: Use your fingernail to scratch a message on the inside part of your forearm. Do not break the skin. The words will appear lighter than your skin color for a moment and then disappear. Later, when you wish to reveal the message, rub your arm briskly and the words will appear in blood-red letters.

The fix: When you scratch your arm you are scraping away dead skin cells. Brisk rubbing of the arm increases heat at that spot and stimulates the blood flow. The letters of the message appear red because the skin over them is thinner and more transparent than the skin that has not been scraped. The blood shows through. Your secret message still will be readable ten or fifteen minutes after you have written it.

A TASTELESS TRICK
Bet you can fool your taste buds!

The setup: Hold your nose and put some dry coffee in your mouth. Can you identify the coffee taste? Chew it. Let it dissolve on your tongue. Roll it around in your mouth. Do anything . . . but don't let go of your nose.

The fix: You'll be fooled, all right. Taste buds aren't what identify coffee flavor. Our sense of smell is the coffee detective. Prove it by letting go of your nose. Coffee is instantly recognizable in the nose and surprisingly in the mouth, too.

Only a few flavors—sweet, salt, sour, and bitter—are detected by the taste buds alone. Without smell, some things like coffee are not recognizable and other tastes are confusing.

2

TRICKY MATTER

Want to be let in on the biggest get-rich-quick scheme of all time? Sure you do. Well, it was not the plunder of King Tut's tomb or an attempt to break into Fort Knox. But it did have to do with gold. The plan was to take all kinds of cheap metals and turn them into gold.

This bright idea was worked on back in the Middle Ages by men called alchemists. The only trouble was, it didn't work. They took all kinds of matter and burned them, boiled them, beat them, and mixed them together. But no matter what they did, they never made gold. Their work was not a total loss, though. They discovered many of the properties of matter.

Modern chemists began where the alchemists left off. Modern chemists didn't make gold either, but a lot of money was made with materials they discovered. Some properties of matter can let you do surprising things. Discover them. You'll be richer for it.

BOUND TO WIN
Bet you can make a ball perform a delayed leap!

The setup: Cut an old tennis ball in half. You can use scissors after you have punctured the ball with a knife. Cut around one of the half balls until you have a two-inch diameter. Turn the disc inside out. Set it on the ground inside out so the dome is up. Wait.

The fix: Suddenly and explosively, the piece of ball will fly into the air. When you retrieve it you will notice it has turned itself right side out again. It will take a little experimenting with the size of the disc and kind of ball to use. If the disc is too small you will not even have time to get your hand away before it performs its inside-out leap. If the disc is too large, it might take hours before the flying leap occurs.

Rubber is a substance made up of long molecules that are folded in accordion fashion. Each molecule acts like a spring. For this reason, rubber has the very interesting property of springing back to its original shape when it has been distorted. This elastic property gives rubber its bounce. This stunt will give you a kick.

QUITE A RIBBING
Bet you can balance a sheet of newspaper on its edge!

The setup: Crease a sheet of newspaper across its diagonal. Fold back each side about an inch from the crease to form a rib, as shown in the picture. Now the newspaper will stand up on edge when you balance it on your hand.

The fix: Folding materials often makes them stronger by deflecting and diverting force. Engineers and architects make use of this fact in the design and construction of buidlings. Another common use is the corrugated (or folded) paper used in boxes. Even animals, like bees, are aware of the fact that the shape of a structure affects the strength of the building material. A honeycomb cell makes wax stronger.

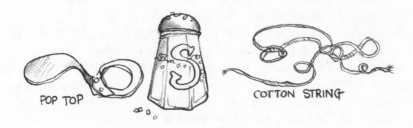

POP TOP

COTTON STRING

ASHES, ASHES, WE DON'T FALL DOWN
Bet you can hang a pop top on ashes!

The setup: Since this stunt uses fire, check with an adult before performing it. Soak about a foot of cotton string in a solution of one tablespoon salt in a half cup of water. (Heat the solution until almost all the salt is dissolved.) Remove the string and let it dry. Cut a length of string about six inches long. Tie one end to the ring of a soft-drink pop top.

Make a stand out of a wire coat hanger by bending the curved hook so it is at right angles to the triangular part. The triangle is placed flat on the table as a base.

Place the hanger stand on a fireproof surface like a stove top or in the sink. Tie the free end of the salt string to the hook with the pop top hanging down. All set? Now, light the string.

The fix: The string flames away and burns out. The pop top is left hanging by the ash. The ash is strengthened by the salt crystals, which don't burn but give the minerals left in the cotton ashes just enough strength to cling together. Don't breathe heavily on the structure. Ashes are not your basic strong suport.

SWEETNESS AND LIGHTNESS

Bet you can make a sugar cube float!

The setup: This is a "do ahead" trick because it takes a bit of doctoring to make a sugar cube float. At the drugstore buy some New Skin, which athletes use to cover blisters. It is mostly a chemical called collodion. Pour some of the New Skin into a small paper cup. Hold the sugar cube with tweezers, dip it completely into the collodion, and hold it there for about twenty seconds. Remove it and set it in a warm place to dry. Wait about twenty-four hours before attempting to "float" it.

Drop an untreated sugar cube into some hot water or tea. It sinks and lies on the bottom of the glass until it dissolves. Now drop your treated cube into the water. Disappointment! It drops to the bottom too. But don't despair. It will slowly surface and float like a cork.

The fix: Collodion has the ability to coat the surface of the sugar crystals both inside and out. It fills in the spaces in the cube. So when the cube is put into hot water, the sugar dissolves but the collodion framework remains behind, and it is buoyant enough to float. And the bonus is it still looks just like a sugar cube. Don't, however, try to eat it.

LEAKPROOF

Bet you can stab a pencil through a water bomb without "exploding" it!

The setup: Fill a polyethylene bag with water. (Make sure it says "polyethylene" on the box.) Twist it closed with a rubber band. Now stab a sharp pencil through the water bomb so that it goes in one side and out the other. Leave the pencil in place. Despite the fact you have made two pencil-size holes, not one drop of water leaks out.

The fix: Polyethylene is a thermoplastic (one that melts with heat) that has the peculiar property of shrinking its molecules together when it is torn. When you puncture the bag with the pencil, the polyethylene shrinks around the opening, closing it off so no water escapes. This same property is used to make tires that can't blow out.

SMOKE BUT NO FIRE!

Bet you can make smoke come from your fingertips!

The setup: This is another one of the fire stunts, so you should get the okay of an adult. You will need to use matches. Gather a metal pan and two books of matches. Tear off the striking surface from one of the books of matches. With the cardboard surface up and the striking surface against the metal pan, light the cardboard behind the striking surface and let it burn in the pan. When it has finished burning, you will notice a reddish-brown residue in the pan. Rub this stuff onto the tips of your finger and thumb. Now, when you rub your finger and thumb together, smoke will curl from your fingertips.

The fix: The striking surface of a matchbook contains a compound of red phosphorus that ignites at a low temperature. When you burn the striking surface you release red phosphorus on the surface of the metal. This substance has the strange property of "burning" at a low temperature. The warmth created by rubbing your fingers together sends the smoke signal of oxidation into the air. Truly a magical effect!

DIRT CHEAP
Bet you can make a black nail turn silver!

The setup: Under adult supervision for the fire part of this trick, please! Hold a nail with a pair of pliers. Place it just over a candle flame. The nail removes heat from the flame so the burning is not complete. This is called a "dirty" fire. Some of the unburned material, in the form of carbon, coats the nail. This coating of black powder is called soot. Drop the soot-covered nail into a glass of water. Look at it from the side. Instead of the pitch-black carbon, it gleams like pure silver. Too bad you can't bank on it.

The fix: Carbon is an element that has the peculiar property of attracting air to its surface. When you put it under water, the water does not wet the finely divided carbon soot. A very thin layer of air lies between the water and the soot. This layer of air causes the silvery look.

HANGING BY A THREAD!

Bet you can lift an ice cube with a thread!

The setup: Curl the end of a piece of thread on an ice cube. Sprinkle generously with salt. Wait about a minute. Now lift the cube. The string is frozen to the cube and provides a handy handle.

The fix: Salt lowers the temperature at which ice freezes. The ice near the salt melts. The string now is surrounded by water. The melted ice refreezes because it is surrounded by material at a lower temperature, which removes heat from the water. The thread now is frozen to the cube. This is a short-time operation, though. If you wait too long, the entire cube will melt and you will have only one wet thread.

REKINDLED CANDLE CAPER

Bet you can get a blown-out candle to relight itself!

The setup: This is a fire trick. Do it over aluminum foil to catch drips. And ask a grown-up to supervise.

Light two large candles. Hold them sideways with one flame about an inch and a half above the other. Blow out the lower flame. Hold the candles steady. The lower candle now will relight itself without any help from you.

The fix: This trick won't wait long, so be quick with the candles! When the lower flame is blown out, the hot gases continue to rise as smoke from the extinguished wick. When these gases reach the upper flame, they act as a wick. The flame burns down the gases and relights the lower candle. The fire now has the three ingredients it needs to continue burning: fuel, oxygen, and the kindling point.

NO ATTRACTION HERE

Bet you can "kill" a magnet (so it loses its power of attraction)!

The setup: Put a small magnet on the burner of the stove. (Check with an adult before you do this.) Turn on the burner. Heat the magnet for about five minutes. Turn off the burner and let the magnet cool for about fifteen minutes before you touch it. Now try to pick up some nails or a paper clip.

The fix: The magnet now is as dead as a doornail and just about as magnetic as one. Magnetism is caused by the regular alignment of iron atoms. When you put heat energy into a magnet, you cause the atoms to vibrate. This shakes them out of their magnetic alignment. Magnets can be "killed" using other means too. One is with a sharp blow. Hit the magnet with a hammer and you will jiggle the alignment. High-voltage electric power also will do the job.

TAPE ESCAPE
Bet you can erase a tape recording with a nickle!

The setup: You will need an ordinary tape recorder or a cassette player, and a Canadian nickle. The "gimmick" to this trick is the Canadian nickle. Place it over the recording heads of the tape recorder, press the play button, and the tape will erase or play with so much interference you can't hear the recording.

The fix: Recording tapes are magnetic. They can be disturbed by strong magnetic elements. Everyone knows that iron can be magnetic, but they may not be aware that nickle also is magnetic. There is only one metal that is more magnetic: cobalt. Nickle in an alloy usually loses its magnetic properties. This is why an American nickle won't work in our trick. It doesn't contain enough nickle. Some alloys, like Monel Metal (mostly nickle and copper), which is used in washing-machine drums, will hold a magnet. Put a magnet next to the Canadian nickle and you will feel the strong attraction immediately.

TIGHT WAD

Bet you can stuff two handfuls of cotton into a full glass of water . . . with no spills!

The setup: Fill a juice glass almost to the top with water. Get two large handfuls of cotton. Be sure to use real cotton, not a synthetic material. Put the cotton bit by bit into the glass of water. Fluff each piece as you wet it so it is thoroughly saturated. Water may begin to bulge over the top of the glass, but if you are careful you can get the entire wad packed into the glass without spilling a single drop of the water.

The fix: You can add all that material to an already full glass because cotton fibers are made up of hollow plant cells filled with air. The water penetrates into the hollow areas, displacing the air. There is so little solid material in the cotton that it is able to fit into the glass.

3
ENERGY ODDITIES

It's going to be hard to fool you with energy. You see, your body is a great energy detector. Your eyes are activated by light energy. Your ears are designed to capture sound energy. Your skin lets you know about both heat and electrical energy. And your senses feed you data on the energy of motion. Your vast experience lets you predict how energy will behave.

So how do we get energy foolers? Your senses aren't foolproof. They have limits. We are going to use scientific knowledge about the limits of your senses to trick you. Further, all energy does not behave predictably, so we have gathered some offbeat facts about energy to fool you too.

Your experience tells you that flames do damage. In this chapter you'll meet a flame that doesn't scorch. Your experience tells you that light makes things visible. But we've got a trick that makes something disappear in broad daylight. Your experience tells you that you can detect the direction of a sound. We can move that sound with a dish and stump you.

There's plenty of energy around. We just haven't figured out how to harness most of it. But there's no energy shortage in this chapter. We have captured more than enough to have fun.

HEAVY PRESSURE

Bet you can cut through an ice cube and it will seal itself behind you!

The setup: You will need about ten inches of fine wire, two spoons, a soda bottle, and an ice cube. Wind each end of the wire around a spoon handle. Leave about four inches of wire between the spoons. Rest the ice cube on top of the bottle. Put the middle of the wire across the ice cube and pull down on the spoons. This isn't a quickie. It takes about ten minutes for the wire to pass completely through the ice cube. But the ice cube will be whole again when the wire passes through the bottom.

The fix: Pressure on the wire melts the ice just underneath it. As the wire moves down, the ice melts. Then the water above the wire refreezes as the heat is removed by the surrounding ice.

47

FIREPROOF PAPER
Bet you can boil water in a paper cup!

The setup: Ask for adult approval about the fire. You will need a lit candle, a paper cup half filled with water, and tongs. Hold the cup with the tongs and center the cup over the flame. Water will heat to boiling, and the cup will not burn. Honest.

The fix: It takes three things to make fire: fuel, oxygen, and heat. Remove one of them and burning isn't possible. Everyone knows that a paper cup will ordinarily burn, so fuel is present. Oxygen always is present in the air. So heat must be the missing element. Water removes the heat so quickly that the paper cup never gets hot enough to reach the kindling point, which is the minimum temperature for combustion. Of course, if you wait until all the water has boiled off, the cup will go to blazes.

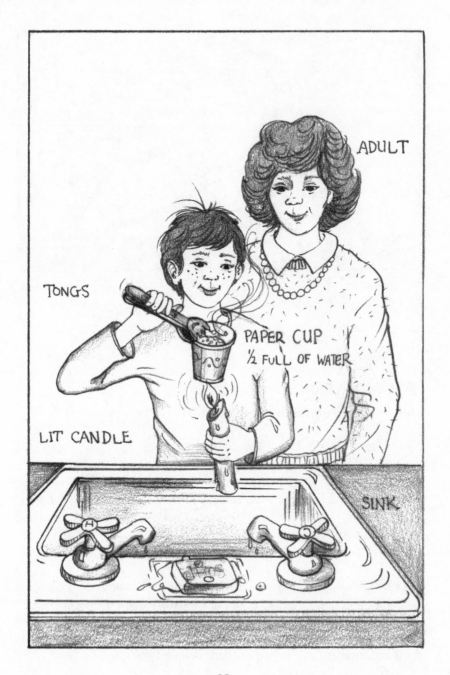

ADULT

TONGS

PAPER CUP
½ FULL OF WATER

LIT CANDLE

SINK

SOUND ADVICE

Bet you can make an echo in a dish!

The setup: You will need two identical soup bowls and a ticking watch. Sit at a table and place one soup bowl in front of you. Hold the other soup bowl upside down over one ear. Hold the watch about an inch above the bottom of the soup bowl on the table. Move your body so that the bowl over your ear is above the bowl on the table. The watch now sounds as if it is ticking in the soup bowl by your ear and not in the one on the table.

The fix: The fix is an echo. Sound bounces off surfaces. Bouncing sounds or echoes can be collected by dish-shaped objects, much as light is collected by the dish-shaped mirrors or antennae of telescopes. The dish shape focuses the echo of the ticking watch. You are hearing the echo, not the original sound.

HEARING AID

Bet you can hear a watch ticking across the room . . . with your ears covered!

The setup: Find a long solid piece of wood, like a dining-room table or a stair rail. Place a watch at one end. Put your ear tightly against the other end. Place your hand over the other ear. Listen.

The fix: You can hear the watch ticking loud and clear. This strange hearing aid really is quite simple. Sound waves travel to your ear more directly through wood than through air because there are fewer things in the way to deflect it. In the air all sorts of currents keep the sound from reaching your ear. So you can hear the watch ticking through the wood when you can't hear it in the air.

LIQUID LAMP

Bet you can pour light!

The setup: You will need a tall, slim jar with a lid (like the kind olives come in), several sheets of newspaper, a flashlight, a hammer, and a large nail. Use the nail and hammer to make two holes in the lid: one large hole near an edge, and a smaller hole near the opposite edge. Fill the jar three-quarters full with water and screw on the lid. Turn on the flashlight and place it at the end of the jar so the light shines into it. Roll both the jar and flashlight in newspaper. (You may need a friend to help you wrap the paper around the two items.) If you are alone we suggest a bit of Scotch tape over the holes until you have the apparatus wrapped securely. The purpose of the newspaper is to make a light-tight tube.

To pour the light, tilt the jar so the water spurts out of the big hole into a basin. Do this in a darkened room. If you stick your finger into the stream of water, light will fall on it. This happens if you put your finger in the water near where it comes out of the jar or in the curved part of the stream near the basin. The light is completely contained in the curved stream of water. Light pours!

The fix: It is true that light travels in a straight line. But there are exceptions to every rule, and this is one of them. The light remains inside the stream of water because it is reflected internally by the water. This phenomenon also occurs in fiber optics, where light is contained in a flexible glass fiber. Fiber optics and the phenomenon of internal reflection can direct light waves anywhere a wire can go. Sending messages on light waves contained in cables of fibers in revolutionizing communications. It can even be used to direct light into dark, small places in the human body during surgery.

A LONG LOOK

Bet you can see to infinity!

The setup: For this truly puzzling trick you will need two mirrors, some modeling clay, and a knife. Use the clay to make a stand so the mirrors can stand vertically. In the center of the back of one mirror, scrape away a circle of silvering with the knife to make a peephole about half an inch in diameter. Set the mirrors parallel to each other a few inches apart, with the reflecting surfaces facing each other. Put an object between them. When you look through the peephole, you will see the image of the object reflected an infinite number of times.

The fix: A mirror is a surface that reflects light. This means that light bounces off it. When such light bounces to another surface that also is reflective, you will see an infinite number of images as long as the mirrors are parallel. If they are at an angle, you'll see a lot of images but at some point the angle will keep you from seeing to infinity.

CLEARLY NOTHING

Bet you can make a glass disappear in a glass!

The setup: You'll need a large glass jar and a smaller one that fits into it easily. Put one jar inside the other. Now fill both the inside jar and the space between jars with paint-and-varnish remover (petroleum distillates). Amazing, the inner jar disappears.

The fix: An object is transparent because light passes through it. Each object has its own particular speed of light transmission. When light travels from one transparent object to another (such as from air to glass), it is bent at the boundary because of the different speeds. Bent light is what lets you see the transparent object.

In this trick you replace air with a transparent liquid (the petroleum distillates) through which light moves at about the same speed as it does through glass. Light doesn't bend at the boundaries, so the boundaries are invisible. Presto! The glass disappears right in front of your eyes.

OUT ON A LIMB

Bet you can fill a stocking with an invisible leg!

The setup: This eerie illusion works best on a cold, dry day. It may not work for you if it's hot and muggy. To make a "ghost" leg you will need a woman's nylon stocking—the shiny kind, not the kind with elastic in it. And you must have a piece of wool (a sweater, sock, or scarf). Hold the toe of the stocking in your left hand. Grasp the piece of wool in your right hand and place it around the stocking close to your left hand. Pull the stocking through the wool-clad hand. Repeat this, rubbing the nylon in the same direction each time. Soon it will be "charged" up. Hold the opening of the stocking in your right hand. It will appear to inflate with an invisible leg.

The fix: Rubbing the nylon gives it an electrical charge known as static electricity. The entire stocking picks up the same charge, and since like charges repel each other, the opposite sides of the stocking move away from each other.

4
FLUID FEATS

MOTHER NATURE'S RULES AND REGULATIONS GOVERNING FLUIDS

State of matter: liquid, gas, and an occasional offbeat solid
Color: any or none
Temperature range: from nearly absolute zero to more than the heat of the sun
Weight of one liter (about a quart): from less than a gram to more than fourteen kilograms (more than thirty pounds)
Time necessary to move one centimeter: from a split second to hundreds of years

Are you thoroughly confused about fluids? We thought you would be. This description of fluids is so strange that it looks like Mother Nature was out to lunch while fluids were being designed. So much the better for creating a challenging puzzle for scientists to unravel.

In the midst of this apparent chaos, there really is strict order. And when you know the rules, you can make fluids behave in extraordinary ways. Some of the most mystifying fluid feats are performed by taking advantage of the fact that all fluids flow . . . unless held in by a container. Some fluids are invisible and exert pressure (as all fluids do) in all directions (pressure that's sometimes hard to notice).

Fluids have forces to be reckoned with. One is their ability to stick together (called *cohesion*), and another is their ability to stick to other materials (called *adhesion*). In this chapter we'll show you some unusual tricks with average fluids: water and air. We won't be dealing with oddball solids like slow-flowing glass or Silly Putty. Common fluids are strange enough.

Don't forget: Fluids are the creepiest things on earth. They creep uphill, downstream, underground, and even creep into each other's spaces. Master them and be king of the creeps.

WATER TOWER
Bet you can lift water in an upside-down glass!

The setup: This is a good trick to do in the bathtub. Fill a tall glass by completely submerging it in water. Get all the air out. Then turn it upside down under the water. Lift it, bottom up, above the surface until only the mouth of the glass is under the water. The water will stay in the glass, rising high above the surface of the bath.

The fix: If you had a taller glass you could lift the water even

higher. You could lift it 33 feet if you had a glass that tall. Air pressure holds up your water tower. There is no air in the glass, so nothing is pressing down on the water in the glass. But air pressure is pressing down on the surface of your bath, and this allows the column of water to rise 33 feet from the surface. An Italian physicist, Torricelli (1608–47), discovered this in 1643. He tried the same trick using mercury, which is 13 times heavier than water. He found that the air pressure could support a column of mercury 760 millimeters high and that this length varied according to the weather. No kidding. On sunny days it was higher than on rainy days. In case you haven't guessed, Torricelli's mercury column was the first barometer, or weather predictor.

INFLATION?

Bet you can lift a dime with a straw!

The setup: Dip the end of a plastic straw in water. Set the straw down on a dime and suck in hard. Lift while inhaling.

Wipe the dime dry and ask a friend to try the trick without water. The dime stays firmly on the table.

The fix: Without water, this trick won't wash! Water makes it work because of several different phenomena. First, the force of adhesion allows the water to be attracted to both the straw and the dime. In addition, water sticks to itself. This is the force of cohesion. And last, water seals the joint so that when you inhale through the straw you reduce the air pressure inside the straw. Air pressure on the underside of the dime pushes it up against the straw. This, combined with the water "glue," is enough force to get your dime off the ground. Too bad its value doesn't go up as well.

GRAB-BAG GRABBER

Bet you can push a plastic bag into a jar so no one can pull it out!

The setup: You could even get the best of King Kong with this trick. It shows that "easy in" does not always mean "easy out." All you need is a plastic bag, a jar with a mouth wide enough for your hand, and a rubber band.

Put the plastic bag inside the wide-mouth jar with the edges of the bag hanging over the mouth of the jar. Make an airtight seal by putting a rubber band over the bag. If the jar has screw ridges, place the rubber band below the ridges. Now try to pull the plastic bag out of the jar.

The fix: The grabber here is air pressure. To pull the bag out of the jar you would have to create a vacuum inside the jar. Human hands are just not strong enough to create this pressure. Nor is the bag strong enough to resist the force needed to pull it from the inside of the jar without tearing. This is a situation where you really are "stuck" for a solution!

COLD-BOILED

Bet you can "boil" water without heat!

The setup: For this weird illusion you will need a small handkerchief and a juice glass about three-quarters full of cold water. Wet the center of the handkerchief and stretch it over the mouth of the glass. Push the wet cloth so it curves slightly into the glass. Now cover the mouth of the handkerchief-covered glass with your right palm.

Grasp the glass with your left hand near its mouth. Turn the glass upside down with your left hand, keeping the mouth tightly pressed to your right palm. Hold the glass and handkerchief firmly and lift the glass off your right hand.

To make the water "boil," press down on the bottom of the glass with your right hand and slide the handkerchief up the sides of the glass with your left hand. As the handkerchief tightens on the mouth of the glass, bubbles form and come to the surface. It looks as if the water is boiling.

The fix: Of course, the water really isn't boiling. But it does give a very good imitation of it. When the glass of water is inverted, a partial vacuum is created in the space above the water. When you tighten the handkerchief across the mouth, air rushes into the glass through the holes in the cloth to fill the vacuum. This produces the bubbles that make the water appear to be boiling.

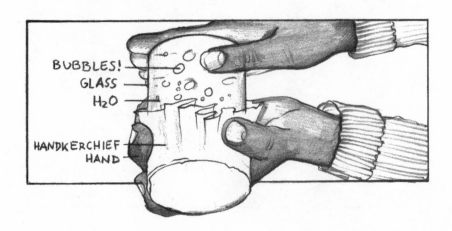

BUBBLES!
GLASS
H₂O
HANDKERCHIEF
HAND

CORK SCREWY

Bet you can sink a cork without touching it!

The setup: Float a perfectly normal cork in a bowl of water. Never at any time will your hands touch the cork, but still you can make it sink below the surface of the water. You need only a large glass.

The fix: The secret sinker here is air! Turn the glass upside down and carefully lower it into the water over the cork. As it sinks below the surface of the water, so does the cork. The water level in the glass is lowered by the compressed air, and the water level of the bowl is increased. Soon you will have a cork "floating" underwater. A sneaky feat if ever there was one!

PROTECTIVE COVERING

Bet you can put a piece of paper underwater without getting it wet!

The setup: Stuff a tissue into the bottom of a six- or eight-ounce glass. The tissue should stay in place when you turn the glass upside down. Now hold the glass perfectly straight in an upside-down position and submerge it into a basin of water. Remove the glass and feel the tissue. It's nice and dry, in spite of its trip.

The fix: Air is the protective covering in this stunt. As you lower the glass into the water, there is no way for the air to escape. The water presses up against it, and the gas compresses. This makes it push back against the water. So the tissue remains dry.

A diving bell works on this principle. Divers take an air supply with them in a bell-shaped container over their heads. They can stay underwater as long as the diving bell doesn't tip and fill with water and they don't go so deep that all the air is squeezed into a tiny space where they can't fit their nose.

DRY CLEANING

Bet you can make a dry spot in two liquids!

The setup: Put a tablespoonful of water on a china saucer. Color it if you wish with a few drops of food coloring. Pour a few drops of rubbing alcohol in the center of the water. Lo and behold, the water rushes away from the alcohol, leaving a dry spot in the center of the plate.

The fix: This stunt is a battle between the "skins" of two liquids. If you don't believe that water has a skin, then watch the baglike drop form on a faucet. The shape of the drop is due to surface tension in the "skin," where the water molecules cling together with quite remarkable strength. Alcohol also has a visible surface tension, but it is not as strong as that of water. On the shallow dish where the two surfaces meet, there is a tug-of-war between the surface tension of alcohol and the surface tension of water. Since the surface tension of water is stronger, it pulls away from the alcohol and destroys the weak surface film of the alcohol, leaving an empty and quite dry spot behind.

I CAN'T BELIEVE I DID THE "HOLE" THING!
Bet you can hold water in a sieve!

The setup: A metal strainer, some clear paraffin wax (the kind used for sealing jelly jars), a double boiler out of an aluminum pan, a larger pot of water, and a piece of paper. You need to use the stove for this trick, so check with an adult first.

Put the paraffin in the pan and melt the paraffin over hot water in the pot. When it is completely melted, quickly dip the sieve into it. Shake the sieve as you remove it so the holes don't fill up with wax. Let the wax harden around the wires.

Put a piece of paper into the bottom of the sieve as you pour cold water into it. The paper breaks the force of the falling water. When you have filled the sieve about halfway, remove the paper. There are many holes, but the water mysteriously stays inside.

The fix: The sieve holds water because the water doesn't wet the waxed surface, and each tiny hole is sealed by the surface tension of the water. The combined surface tension of all the holes is enough to keep the water in the sieve. This works only when the holes are small.

NOTHING TO SNEEZE AT

Bet you can part a pepper sea!

The setup: Fill a glass or a bowl with water and sprinkle pepper liberally on the top. Stroke a path through the pepper with your index finger and try to make the pepper "clear the road."

The fix: You can't do this unless you first coat your finger with soap. The soapy finger then will make a clean sweep through the floating pepper. Soap weakens the surface tension of the water, and the pepper no longer is able to float on the surface but sinks into the water below.

WATER ON A TIGHTROPE
Bet you can pour water sideways!

The setup: Wet a string about three feet long and tie it to the handle of a pitcher or measuring cup. Fill the pitcher about two-thirds full of water. Pass the string from the handle over the mouth of the pitcher and down the spout to a glass about two feet to the side of the pitcher. Hold the pitcher a foot off the table. With your left hand hold the end of the wet string inside the glass. Not a drop will spill on the table!

The fix: There are two forces with you here. One is the attraction between the water and the surface of the string. Water wets the string and sticks to itself. The attraction of water for itself creates a stream. Together these two forces are greater than gravity, which is pulling the water toward the ground.

LOOK, MA—NO HANDS
Bet you can keep a ball in the air for an hour!

The setup: All you need to perform the seemingly impossible is a Ping-Pong ball and a hair dryer. Turn on the dryer and hold it so that the stream of air is pointing straight up. Place a Ping-Pong ball in the stream of air. It doesn't blow away but sits so securely that you can move the hair dryer to an almost horizontal position.

You don't really have to hold the hair dryer for an hour to see that this trick is going to work. A few minutes is long enough to see this spectacular effect.

But if you really want an even bigger show, try floating several items in the airstream at the same time. Put a Ping-Pong ball closest to the dryer, then add a balloon and over that a beachball or a larger balloon weighted with paper clips. See how long a line of floaters you can manage.

The fix: The invisible ballplayer is air. In this case what you see is the result of the Bernoulli effect. Bernoulli, an Italian physicist who lived in the eighteenth century, discovered a peculiar property of moving fluids. He showed that moving air exerts less pressure in a direction at right angles to its motion than still air does. This means that air from the dryer moves faster around the side of the ball than air moving on top of the ball, which is still. So the air pressure sits heavier on top of the ball and holds it in its midair float. The Bernoulli effect is the reason that heavier-than-air planes fly. Air rushing over the tops of wings exerts less pressure than air under the wings does. Thus, the under air pushes up to give planes a lift.

THE BURNING QUESTION
Bet you can make ashes float in the air!

The setup: Fire is used in this stunt, so check with an adult before trying it. You will need lightweight tissue paper, scissors, rubber cement, and an aluminum pit pan. Make sure you have plenty of cleared space on the table or countertop, and nothing above it (for instance, a wall-mounted cabinet or a lamp) that could be damaged by the flame, maoke, or ash.

Cut the paper into a rectangle about five by eight inches. Roll the paper into a tube that is eight inches high and about two inches in diameter. Secure the paper with a few dabs of rubber cement. Set the tube in the middle of an aluminum pie pan so it looks like a little chimney. Set fire to the paper at the top of the tube. The tube will burn quickly downward. As it nears the bottom, the black, tube-shaped ash will rise into the air. Some people call this the phoenix trick, because the phoenix was a mythical bird that rose into the air from its own ashes.

The fix: The tube shape causes a column of hot air to form inside the column. Since warm air rises, this column of superheated air will pull up the lightweight ash. Rising warm air is called a convection current. The "lifting power" of the small amount of hot air you have created is not very strong. That is why you have to use extremely lightweight paper. This trick sometimes works with different-size tubes and with various kinds of paper. This is fun to experiment with.

5

MECHANICAL MARVELS

The force is with you. Mechanical force, that is. You have taken advantage of mechanics most of your life. Use a screw, a tennis racket, or a bicycle and you've got a mechanical advantage. It's no mystery that these devices can make you stronger or faster.

The challenges in this chapter put you at a mechanical disadvantage. Forces are working against you. It will take mechanical marvels to set the odds back in your favor. You'll discover them . . . and in the strangest places, too. We'll place them at your fingertips. In fact, your fingertips *are* mechanical marvels. And you can get help defying gravity from a grain of rice.

Mechanics is the study of force and the motion it causes. Our mechanical marvels manipulate forces. You'll even be able to hold off a whole gang when the force is with you. We invite you to try mechanics. Don't make us resort to force!

STACKED ODDS

Bet you can remove only the bottom checker of a stack without touching it!

The setup: Stack eight checkers on a smooth surface. Strike the bottom checker briskly with the edge of a table knife.

The fix: The bottom checker snaps out and the stack remains stacked, just one checker shorter.

There is a law of physics that explains this trick: the law of inertia. An object at rest will remain at rest unless acted upon by an outside force. In this case the knife exerts the outside force but *only to the bottom checker.* The only force acting on the rest of the stack is friction. If the bottom checker moves off fast enough, the friction is so small that it has no noticeable effect on the rest of the stack.

The same principle is in effect here as in the trick where you pull a tablecloth out from under a fully set table. If you really are good with the checker gimmick, then you might set your sights on the tablecloth.

STRONG-ARM TACTICS
Bet you can hold off ten people!

Your secret ally, science, will enable you to keep ten strong people from pushing you against a wall.

The setup: Place your palms against the wall, fingers pointing up, arms outstretched. Brace yourself. Have your ten people line up behind you, each one with hands on the shoulders of the person

before him or her. At a signal, everyone pushes with all their strength to press you to the wall.

The fix: You won't fold. You will withstand them all. The reason is that each person absorbs the force of the one directly behind him or her so there is no cumulative force. As long as you can withstand the force of the person directly behind you, you can beat the whole lineup. As a sneaky precaution, choose the weakest one to stand directly behind you.

GETTING DOWN
Bet you can keep a friend in a chair with one finger!

The setup: Have a friend sit in a chair chin up, head back. Put your index finger against the forehead and press. Tell your friend to try to get up.

The fix: Your friend is now a prisoner at your fingertip. In a resting position the center of gravity of the body (the point at which all weight seems to be centered) is located over the place where it rests (the base). In a seated position the center of gravity is over the seat. In order to stand, the center of gravity must shift to over the feet. The head *must* move forward to make this shift. The slight pressure against the forehead is just enough to keep your friend sitting tight.

FRIENDLY GET-TOGETHER
Bet you can outtug a tug-of-war!

The setup: You can outpull four big people with this stunt. No kidding. You will need two broomsticks and about twenty feet of strong rope. This trick can be done with two or four other people. Our directions are for two people. Have both people hold a broomstick in front of them. They should stand about three feet apart. Tie the end of the rope securely to one broomstick about a foot from the end. Wind it around both broomsticks about five times. Be sure the rope does not cross itself at any time. You hold the end of the rope next to one of the broomstick holders. When you give the signal, the holders try to keep the two broomsticks from coming together while you pull on the rope. Much to everyone's amazement, they will not be able to resist your force. You will pull the tug-of-war together single-handedly. This

trick is even more impressive with four people (two on each broomstick team).

The fix: Mother Nature is giving you a mechanical advantage here. You are setting up a pulley system. Pulleys are simple machines that change the direction of force. A single change of direction doesn't make a job easier, but when you change direction more than once, you have gained a mechanical advantage. When you wrap the rope around the broomsticks you have four changes of direction, so you can multiply your pulling power by four.

Let's say that everyone exerts a force of fifty pounds. The tug-of-war is at a stalemate, with equal amounts pulling against each other. You give one team (the one pulling in the same direction you are) an advantage with your force. It tips the balance and you win. Yea!

FAKIR FAKEOUT

Bet you can lift a jar of rice with a knife!

The setup: You will need a jar with a narrow mouth (we used a mayonnaise jar), uncooked rice, and a large carving knife. Fill the jar to the brim with rice. Stab in it quickly a number of times with the knife. The level of rice goes down because the stabbing causes the grains to pack together tightly. Add rice to the jar to keep it filled. After twenty or thirty stabs give a quick, long thrust into the rice with the knife. The knife will stick into the rice and you can lift the entire jar with the knife handle.

The fix: The preliminary knife stabs rearrange the rice grains so they become packed tightly enough to press against the knife blade with a force that will allow you to lift the jar into the air.

We called this trick fakir fakeout because it is a common stunt performed by Indian fakirs or magicians.

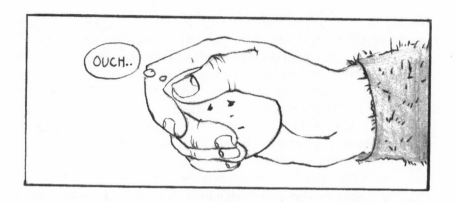

TOUGH SHAPE

Bet you can squeeze a raw egg without breaking it!

The setup: This squeeze play is simple. Be certain that when you squeeze, your hand completely surrounds the egg and you put pressure evenly on all sides. That's all the gimmick there is. Just make sure you're not wearing a ring and there are no cracks in the eggshell.

The fix: Believe it or not, an egg is cleverly designed to withstand force. The oval shape of an egg is extremely strong when forces are applied evenly to it. Uneven forces crack it, so do this over a sink just to be on the safe side.

For a fun variation, try supporting some heavy books on eggshell halves. Crack two raw eggs in half. (Eat the contents as scrambled eggs.) Wash out the shells and trim them with scissors to remove any jagged edges. Set the four shells, dome side up, on a table under the four corners of a very heavy book. See how many books you can add to the eggshell tower. Bet you'll be surprised at the results.

BURNING A CANDLE AT BOTH ENDS
Bet you can make a candle seesaw by itself!

The setup: Peel the wax off the bottom end of a birthday candle to expose the wick. Stick a long sewing needle through the candle so it is centered on the needle. Set two glasses on some aluminum foil and rest the ends of the needle on the rims of the glasses. The foil is there to catch the drips. Make sure the candle is close to horizontal before you proceed.

Ask the okay of an adult before you light both ends of the candle. Watch it seesaw back and forth as if it had a life of its own. Truly an amazing stunt.

The fix: There is almost no chance that the candle will burn evenly at both ends. As the burning progresses one end gets lower, wax drops from it, and it rises in reaction to the sudden weight loss. This begins the seesaw motion, which continues as the lower side drops wax, and the pattern begins again. This simple back-and-forth exchange is called harmonic motion. A common example is a pendulum swinging back and forth.

Now you know the ups and downs of burning a candle at both ends.

IN ORBIT

Bet you can make a ball defy gravity!

The setup: We can tell you how to keep a ball in an upside-down jar even when there is no lid. You will need a Ping-Pong ball and a large jar with a narrow mouth. A mayonnaise jar or a pickle jar is great. Place the ball on a table and put the mouth of the up-side-down jar over the ball. Hold the jar by the bottom and rotate it rapidly with a wrist motion. The ball will move around and around the inside of the jar. As the motion speeds up, the ball will climb the sides of the jar. Lift the rotating jar off the table. The ball will stay in the jar until you stop the motion.

The fix: With a flick of your wrist you set the ball in orbit. The circular motion of your hand creates a force that makes the ball hug the walls of the jar. If the jar disappeared, the ball would fly off in a straight line. The motion imitates the orbit of a planet around the sun. In nature, the paths of the planets are the result of two forces. One is gravity, which pulls the planet and the sun together, and the other is the motion, or momentum, of the planet, which would send it off into space. The two forces combine to produce a fairly circular orbital path. The minute you stop your motion, gravity will take over and the ball will fall out the hole.

6

GEOMETRY GRABBERS

And now for a word from the math department. WAIT! Don't close the book. We promise you won't have to do any adding, subtracting, multiplying, or dividing. And except for one trick, you won't even have to count.

Here's what you are going to do: cut, slice, twist, and bend. Doesn't sound much like math, does it? But these are the kinds of things you do in geometry, the part of mathematics that deals with shapes and surfaces.

We're especially fascinated with the branch of geometry known as topology. Topologists are concerned with the things that remain the same about a surface or shape no matter how much you squeeze or twist it. To topologists a human being has a shape equal to that of a doughnut. They also claim that you can't get all the hairs on a furry ball to lie flat. There will be two spots where the hairs point away from each other. And topologists gave mapmakers a hand when they discovered you only need four colors to make any map, no matter how complicated the map.

Geometry was invented to measure the earth. These challenges aren't quite so difficult, but you will have fun solving them. We're counting on it.

LOST AND FOUND

Bet you can make 65 squares out of 64!

The setup: Get some graph paper and cut it as shown in diagram A. Notice that there are 8 squares along each adjacent side. You can figure the total number of squares as 8 × 8 or 64.

Now rearrange the cut pieces as shown in diagram B. You now have 5 squares on one side and 13 on the adjacent side. Figuring the area as before, you have 5 × 13 or 65 squares. You get an extra square free.

The fix: This trick actually requires cheating. In the rearranged pieces it looks as if the two corners were made by parts with right angles. Actually they aren't. The pieces don't fit exactly, although the figure appears to be square.

Bet you can get 63 squares from 64 with nothing left over!

The setup: This is a companion to the other trick with squares, but in this one we will make a square disappear. Cut the graph paper as shown in diagram A and reassemble it as in diagram C.

The fix: The fix is the same here. With your little deception you can make a whole square appear and disappear at will.

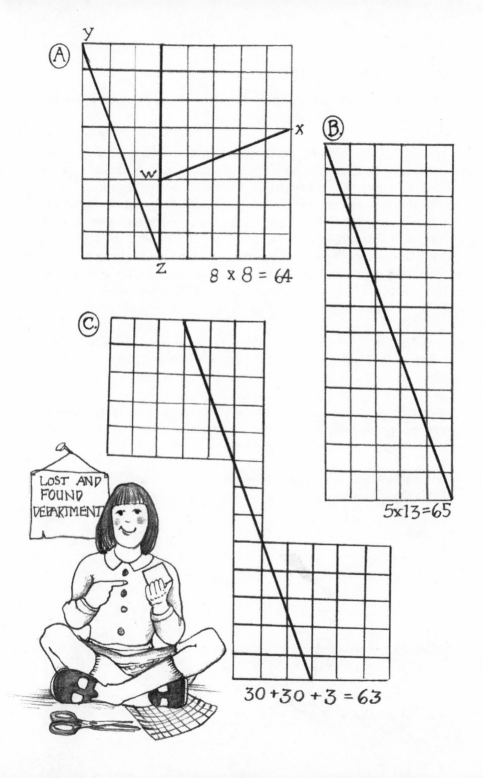

A

y

x

w

z

$8 \times 8 = 64$

B

$5 \times 13 = 65$

C.

LOST AND
FOUND
DEPARTMENT

$30 + 30 + 3 = 63$

AN INSIDE JOB

Bet you can slice a banana without peeling it—and without using a knife!

The setup: For this slippery operation you will need a ripe banana, a needle, and a thread. Stick the threaded needle into a spot on one ridge of the banana and bring it out at the next ridge. Pull the thread taut but leave a three- or four-inch tail sticking out of the original hole. Push the needle back into the second hole and bring it out at the next ridge. Repeat until you have gone completely around the banana. Then hold both ends of the thread in your hand and pull the thread completely free of the banana. For a really special surprise, make more "secret slices." Peel . . . and eat your experiment.

The fix: This trick looks much more difficult than it really is. The principle behind the slicing is simple. All the fancy sewing has merely run a circle of thread around the outside of the fruit inside the skin. The thread is strong enough to act as a knife and to cut through the soft flesh of the banana. This is a math maneuver called sectioning.

101

GRAND OPENING
Bet you can pass your body through a 3 × 5 card!

The setup: Fold an index card down the middle lengthwise. Cut it as shown in the picture. Finally, cut along the fold from x to x, leaving the two folded ends uncut.

The fix: Open the card and you'll find a ring large enough to pass over your body. The circumference of the ring is equal to the lengths of all the cuts you have made. What is really strange is that you have made a circle out of a lot of straight lines.

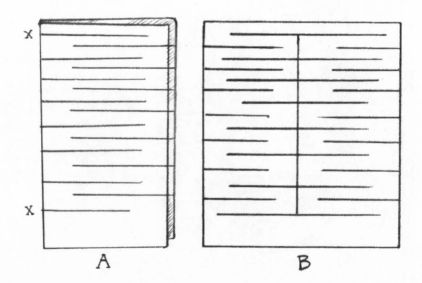

AN ENDLESS JOB

Bet you can type on two sides of a piece of paper without taking it out of the typewriter!

The setup: Cut a one-inch strip from the length of a regular piece of typing paper. Stick one end through the roller of the type-writer. Place it close to the middle. Twist one end of the paper and tape the ends together to make a flat seam. Type a letter or two, go down a few lines, and type some more under the original letters. Keep going around and you will come to the starting letters. Open the loop and take it from the machine. There is typing on both sides.

The fix: The twisted loop you created is called a Möbius strip, named after a famous nineteenth-century German mathematician. The twist in the loop gives it a peculiar property: There is only one surface, although there appear to be two. Möbius strips are fun to cut in half lengthwise. Make a long loop out of a strip of newspaper. Cut it down the middle for a surprise.

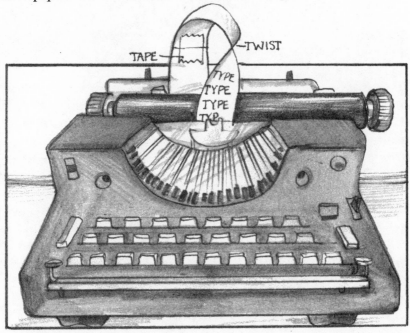

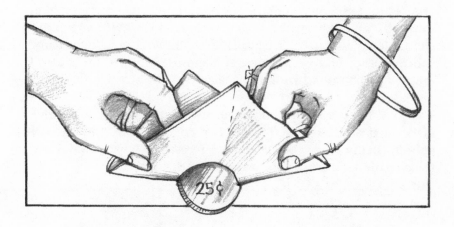

LOOSE CHANGE

Bet you can pass a quarter through a hole the size of a dime!

The setup: Cut a hole the size of a dime in the center of a piece of paper. Try to slip a quarter through the hole without tearing the paper. Won't fit? It will if you fold the paper in half; place the quarter in the fold; and bend the paper upward as you grip it at the outer edges of the crease. With a little manipulation the quarter will slip right through the dime-size hole.

The fix: It's topology again. This numberless math deals with surfaces. Folding the paper enables you to distort the circle to an ellipse. An ellipse is a shape that is like a circle. Topologically it is the same. It has a short diameter and a long diameter. The quarter slips through the long diameter in a stunt that is baffling because we convert a two-dimensional shape into a 3-D one.

GRIPPING ACTION
Bet you can knot a string without letting go of the ends!

The setup: Set a piece of string about a foot long on the table in front of you. Fold your arms across your chest. With your arms still folded, grasp the left end of the string with your right hand, and the other end with your free hand. Hang on to the ends of the string and unfold your arms. Surprise! The string is knotted.

The fix: This is a math trick, believe it or not. The gimmick that makes it possible is called transfer of curves. Your arms had the knot in them before you picked up the string. What you did was transfer the knot from your arms to the string.

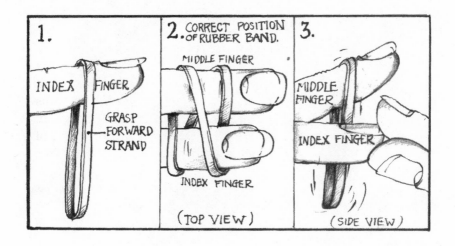

| 1. INDEX FINGER | 2. CORRECT POSITION OF RUBBER BAND. | 3. |
| GRASP FORWARD STRAND | MIDDLE FINGER INDEX FINGER (TOP VIEW) | MIDDLE FINGER INDEX FINGER (SIDE VIEW) |

THE GREAT ESCAPE

Bet you can make a rubber band jump from one finger to another!

The setup: Hang a rubber band over the index finger of your left hand. Take the free end in your other hand and turn the loop so that one strand is forward. Pull the band down and around the middle finger. It is important that the strand that is forward on the index finger also be forward on the middle finger (see the diagram). Now loop the band over the top of the middle finger and place it on the end of the index finger.

Grasp the end of your index finger with your right hand and bend your middle finger. The band will snap free of the index finger and hang on your middle finger. Mysterious.

The fix: Topology tricks you here too. It appears that your index finger is completely tied up. It is not. The rubber band is looped so that the middle finger opens the circle. The loops on the index finger appear to be the edges of the circle but they actually are the middle.

INDEX

VICKI COBB, a New York City native, received her bachelor's degree in zoology from Barnard College and her master's degree in secondary science education from Columbia University. She has written many science-related books for young readers, and was the creator and host of "The Science Game," a television show. Ms. Cobb lives in Mamaroneck, New York.

KATHY DARLING was born in Hudson, New York, but has lived in more than thirty countries and, as a child, attended more than forty schools. She received her bachelor of science degree from Russell Sage College. Ms. Darling has been an editor and author of children's books, a syndicated columnist, and president and publisher of a small, specialty publishing company. She lives in Larchmont, New York.

STELLA ORMAI was born in Bethlehem, Pennsylvania, and both of her parents were artists. She received a bachelor of fine arts from Rhode Island School of Design, where she majored in illustration. She lives with her husband in Providence, Rhode Island.